READING ABOUT

Ancient
Greeks

Jim Pipe

Aladdin/Watts
London • Sydney

Contents

© Aladdin Books Ltd 2000

Designed and produced by
Aladdin Books Ltd
28 Percy Street
London W1P 0LD

First published in
Great Britain in 2000 by
Franklin Watts
96 Leonard Street
London EC2A 4XD

ISBN 0 7496 3908 3
A catalogue record for this
book is available from the
British Library.

Printed in Belgium

All rights reserved

Editor
Mark Jackson

Historical Consultant
Peter Derow

Series Literacy Consultant
Wendy Cobb

Design
Flick Killerby Book Design and Graphics

For Hugh

Who Were the Greeks?

The Ancient Greeks lived in Greece over 2,500 years ago. That's a very long time when you think that the oldest car was built only about 110 years ago. But in lots of ways, the Ancient Greeks were very modern.

Many of them lived in cities with markets, bars, schools and theatres. They had doctors, police officers, law-makers and scientists.

The Greeks held the first Olympic Games about 2,800 years ago.

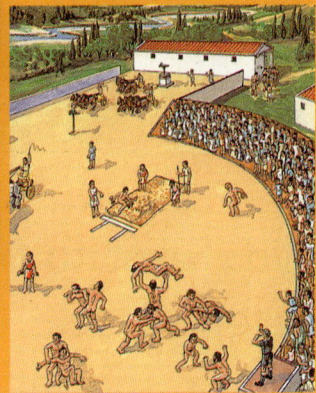

This Greek temple, called the Parthenon, still stands in Athens.

Can you see it in the picture on page 5?

We are still using lots of Greek ideas and inventions. Modern buildings still have columns like Ancient Greek temples. Children learn Greek mathematics in schools all over the world.

Everyday we use Ancient Greek words like cinema, radio, poetry and drama. We also read about Greek heroes like Theseus and Heracles (also known as Hercules).

If you want to find out about how the Ancient Greeks lived, and what made them so special, then read on!

Ancient Greece

Where Was It? • Cities • Travel and Trade

This is the city of Athens about 2,300 years ago. It was the richest city in Ancient Greece and its people were very proud of their fine temples and buildings.

Ancient Greece

Athens was one of hundreds of Greek cities. On the map above, some of the most important cities are marked with red dots.

Ancient Greece wasn't one country like it is now. Each Greek city was like a tiny country, and it included all the farms and villages nearby. The cities often fought each other.

Some cities were on the Greek islands. Others were on the coast of Asia Minor (now Turkey) and around the Mediterranean Sea.

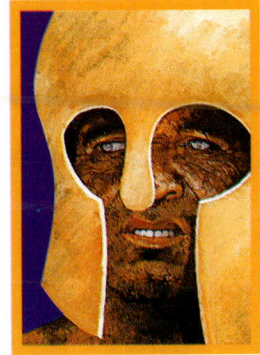

A Greek soldier

All Greeks spoke the same language and believed in the same gods. Anyone who did not speak Greek was a "barbarian", because their words sounded like "bar, bar" to the Greeks.

The most famous barbarians were the Persians. They came from the area that is now Iraq and Iran. They attacked Greece with a big army twice. But both times the Greeks beat them.

Many cities were cut off from each other by high mountains. But nowhere in Greece is far from the sea. The writer Plato said the Greeks lived around the sea like frogs around a pond.

So sailing was the easiest way to travel. The Greeks sailed all over the Mediterranean Sea. Some travellers were traders, others went to build a new home for themselves.

Greek ships, called galleys, had sails. But when there was no wind, up to 200 men rowed them.

The traders brought back corn, metals, wood and slaves. They also brought ideas from other ancient peoples.

Over a long time, the Greeks worked out their own alphabet and mathematics using ideas from the east. They also copied painting and statues from Egypt.

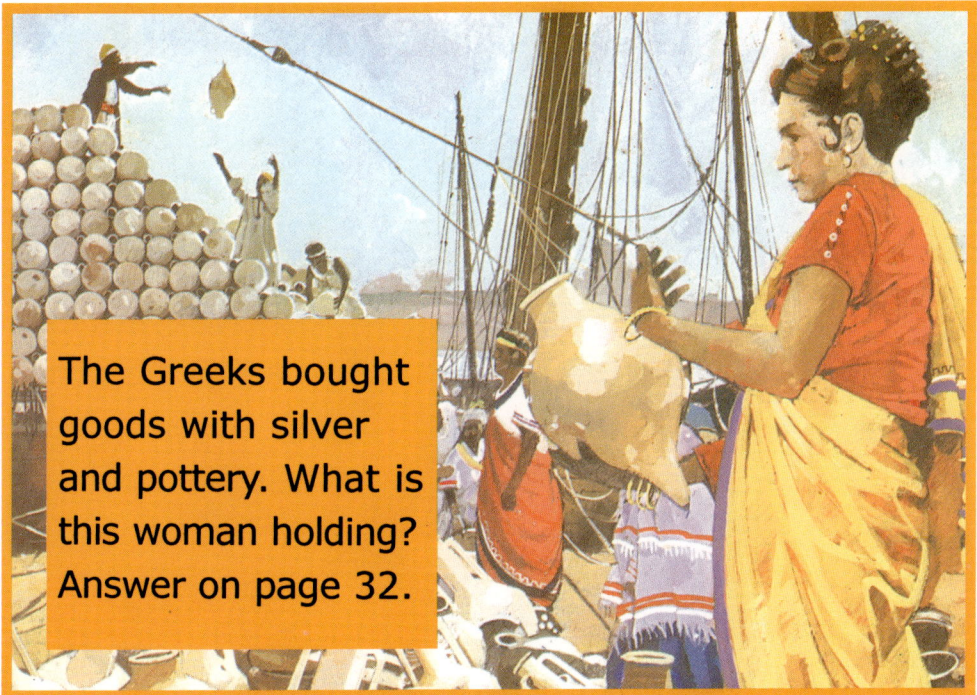

An Ancient Egyptian statue

The Greeks bought goods with silver and pottery. What is this woman holding? Answer on page 32.

Land and People

For most of the year, the weather in Ancient Greece was hot and dry. But the winters were cold and windy. It was a tough place to live.

Most of the flat land for growing crops was near the sea. Here farmers grew wheat, olives and grapes, and vegetables, such as cabbages and onions. They also kept chickens and pigs.

In the hills and mountains, shepherds looked after goats and sheep and kept bees for honey.

Ancient farmers had no tractors. What did they use instead? Answer on page 32.

Greek farmers still use some ancient methods and tools.

The Greeks spent a lot of time out in the sun. They liked to keep fit. If they didn't die in war or from disease, they might reach an old age.

Most Ancient Greeks had dark hair and dark eyes. They were shorter than Greek people today, but they were very strong and tough.

In most cities, you could find a mix of free Greeks, foreigners and slaves. The biggest city, Athens, had over 100,000 people in it.

The most important people in any city were the free Greeks. They had all the best jobs, but they also had to fight for their city.

Rich Greek women only did a few jobs, such as being a priestess. They spent a lot of time at home. Other women worked in the markets.

Most women made the family clothes. Poor women did all the cooking and cleaning too.

Slaves did the jobs no one else liked, like working in the silver mines.

Men spent a lot of their time at work or chatting with their men friends. Having slaves gave rich men lots of free time.

More than half the people in Athens were slaves. Many worked in the fields or in workshops. Even poor people usually had one slave. A rich man might own dozens of them.

There were also foreigners working in Greek cities. The Greeks were probably friendly to them. The ancient Greek word for "stranger" is the same as the word for "guest".

Greek Children

Greek men ruled their families. When a baby was born in Sparta, its father decided if it was healthy. If not, he left it on a hill to die.

Young children had toys such as kites and pottery dolls. In Athens, there was a special day for children. Parents put flowers on their heads and gave them tiny wine jugs as presents.

The Spartans wanted to be tough. Their schools were like army training camps.

Girls were taught at home, and most of them married at at 15. Boys went to school from six to 14. At 18, they joined the army for two years.

At school, boys learned reading, writing and maths. The school day lasted from sunrise to sunset, and there were no long holidays.

Children learned long poems off by heart. Some poems were 26,000 lines long!

Spartan teachers fed their pupils badly and beat them often.

Daily Life

Most of the time, Ancient Greek men and women wore clothes called chitons (say "ky-tons"). But in the hot sun, men often wore very little when they worked.

Rich men and women covered the chitons with wool cloaks or tunics. They folded the cloth in different ways to make new fashions.

Chitons were square pieces of cloth with holes for the arms and head.

The Greeks had all sorts of hairstyles. Spartan men were famous for their curls.

Most of the time the Greeks wore nothing on their feet, though some wore sandals or boots.

Greek houses were also simple. They were made from mud bricks, and had a roof made of tiles. There were few windows — perhaps because the streets were smelly, noisy and dusty.

Most houses had plain walls and a few pieces of wooden furniture. Food was cooked over a fire or in a stone oven, and water came from a well.

Bedroom

Kitchen

Store room

Altar

Men's meeting room

Entrance

Workshop

Coins

The Greeks lived on bread, olives, beans and fruit — and meat if they were rich. They made cheese from sheep's and goat's milk.

People drank wine with most meals. They mixed it with water so it was not too strong.

The market place, or agora. Greece was one of the first places where people used coins.

The Ancient Greeks used wheat and barley to make bread, cakes and porridge.
  They used olive oil for cooking, and honey for making food sweet.

Sparta was famous for its terrible food. One visitor said he understood why the Spartans were so brave. Once you tried their food you didn't mind dying!

Men usually did the shopping in the morning. In big towns, they went to different markets for different goods.

Many goods came from abroad. Wheat came from Egypt and Russia, and cherries from Persia (now Iran). Apricots, peaches and spices came from India and China.

The farmers were the city's soldiers. They fought with swords, spears and shields.

Local goods were often bought from the people who made them. Every Greek town had its own potters, carpenters, shoemakers, jewellers and blacksmiths.

Men from the towns also worked on farms nearby. They gathered wheat in the spring and picked olives and grapes in the autumn.

City Life

Most Greeks were very proud of themselves.
The Spartans thought they were very brave.
The Athenians thought they were clever and
called some of their neighbours "stupid pigs".

Every city thought it had the best people and
ideas. Because of this, the Greeks often fought
each other.

Some cities were ruled by kings or rich men.
But in others, people made their own rules.

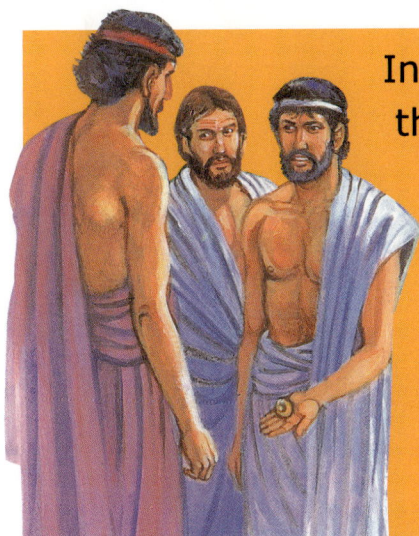

In Athens, ordinary people chose
their leaders and generals.
They also decided if a
criminal was guilty
or not. They voted
with two special
pieces of clay
marked "guilty"
and "not guilty".

On a busy day, 6,000 men went to the big meetings in Athens. But women, slaves and foreigners couldn't take part.

In Athens, most decisions were made at a big meeting that took place every nine days. Any free man could turn up, make speeches or vote.

Each speaker gave his point of view and was timed with a water clock. When the water stopped flowing, the next speaker came on. Then everyone voted by putting their hand in the air.

Good speakers made everyone listen to them. But if a speaker got too powerful, the people could ban him from the city for ten years.

Ancient Athens gave us the word "democracy". It means the "rule of the people" — everyone should be able to take part in running their country.

The Ancient Greeks loved to talk and argue. The men often chatted in sports halls called gymnasia.

Because every Greek city was different, the Greeks thought about how things were done. They asked questions like "What are things made of?" and "What is the best way to live?".

Many ancient peoples blamed gods for things they didn't understand. It was the gods' fault if you got sick or if there was a storm.

Greek inventors living in Egypt built lighthouses and even an early sort of steam engine.

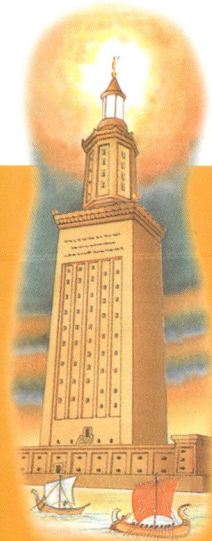

Some Greeks looked for other reasons. They worked out some of the important rules for maths, geography, biology and history.

A Greek scientist called Archimedes invented a machine for raising water. Farmers still use it today.

We still use Ancient Greek ideas. You may have learnt Pythagoras' rule about triangles. Doctors today still follow an Ancient Greek doctor's rules for looking after patients.

Not all Greeks liked clever thinkers. One, called Socrates, was forced to drink poison because people said he was rude to the gods.

Gods and Games

T e m p l e s • **T h e   O l y m p i c s** • **T h e a t r e**

Most Ancient Greeks believed in gods and magic. They thought that if they made the gods happy, it would make life better for them. They were also afraid that an angry god would hurt them.

So the Greeks said prayers at home and took part in festivals. They built beautiful, big temples for the gods to live in.

Priests sacrificed animals as a gift to the gods. At home, people poured wine on an altar.

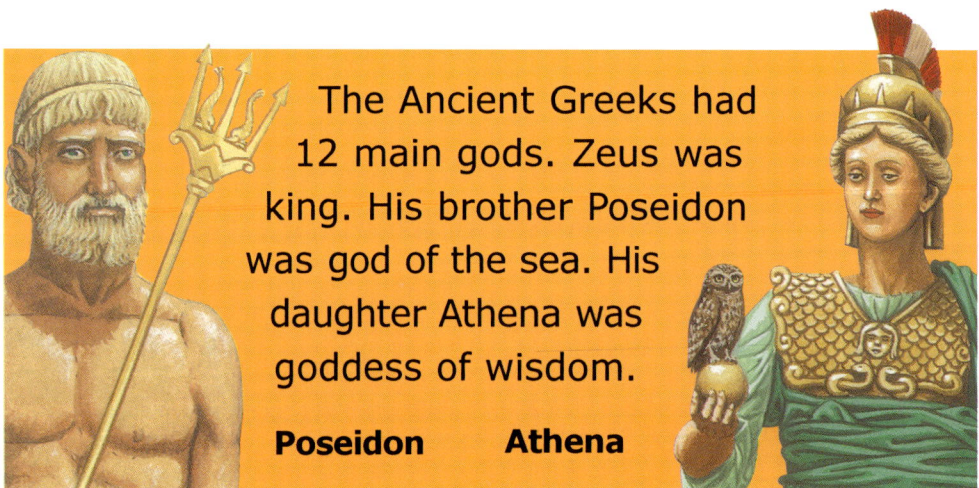

The Ancient Greeks had 12 main gods. Zeus was king. His brother Poseidon was god of the sea. His daughter Athena was goddess of wisdom.

Poseidon   **Athena**

The Greeks also asked the gods about the future. Sometimes they wrote their questions on pieces of lead. They got an answer by listening to the trees.

A present of wine for the gods

At a temple in Delphi, a priestess told people the god Apollo's reply. But her answers were often hard to understand.

Some festivals included sporting events. The most famous were the Olympic Games. Athletes came from all over Greece to take part.

The main events were running, wrestling, boxing and chariot racing. Athletes who won at the Games became heroes in their own city.

In one race the runners wore armour – and not much else!

All the parts in a Greek play were played by men. They wore masks that made their voices louder.

The Olympic Games go on today. But they are not the only Greek idea we still enjoy.

The Greeks also sang and danced to the gods. These dances became the first plays. We still enjoy these plays, along with Ancient Greek sculptures, poems and stories.

Ancient Greek theatres were often built on the side of a hill. The largest theatre held 12,000 people.

Find Out More

Some of the things the Ancient Greeks invented are still around. Can you remember what they are? Below are a few pictures from the book which should give you some clues. Turn to page 32 for the answers.

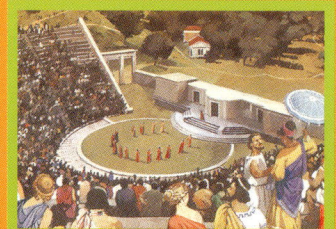

UNUSUAL WORDS

Here we explain some words you may have read in this book.

Agora The market place in the centre of a Greek city.

Barbarian People from other countries, who didn't speak Greek.

Chiton A piece of clothing worn over the body.

Column A tall pillar that holds up the roof. Many Greek temples were built using columns.

Criminal A person who has done a crime, such as stealing money or killing someone.

Democracy "Rule by the people". The Greek idea that everyone should take part in running their city or country.

Galley A Greek ship powered by sails and oars.

Gymnasium A place to exercise. To the Greeks it was also a good place to chat.

History This Ancient Greek word means learning about the past. To the Greeks it meant "finding out" about anything.

Sacrifice An animal that is killed and given to the gods as a present. Greek priests also killed animals to find out the future.

Temple The building where Greek priests prayed to the gods.

Greek Statues

Greek artists were some of the first to create statues that looked like real people (like this athlete). For 2,000 years, many other artists have followed this style.

FAMOUS GREEKS

Alexander the Great

About 2,300 years ago, Greeks from Macedonia beat all the other Greek cities (see map on page 6). Their king, Alexander the Great, led a big Greek

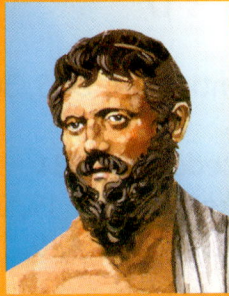

army halfway across the world. He spread Greek ideas from Egypt to India.

Aristotle and Plato (left)

These two thinkers wrote down many important ideas about how people should live. People still study them today.

Archimedes

The Greeks were great at maths. Archimedes worked out how a heavy boat can still float. We use Greek letters in maths today, like π (say "pi").

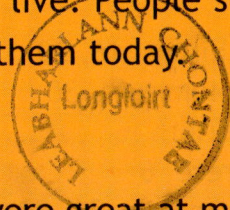

Who Came First?

Egyptians	Greeks	Romans	Vikings	Present Day

4,000 years ago	2,500 years ago	2,000 years ago	1,000 years ago	Now